Small Event Planning

Parties, Vacations, and Weddings on Your Budget!

By

Sara Castellano

Small Event Planning

ISBN: 9781696872744

Warning and Disclaimer

Publisher Contact

Skinny Bottle Publishing

books@skinnybottle.com

Introduction

In my small event planning service, I get a lot of last-minute clients who had the best of intentions for the get-together they started to plan. But it's easy to get overwhelmed, realized you have a week until the party and other deadlines you can't miss, and all you've done is send out the invitations. The RSVPs are laying around somewhere, who knows exactly where anymore, but you have somewhere between 40 and 500 guests and a big crisis descending.

We get this or hear about it from the trenches almost every week. The DIY event you wanted to save money on is now a money pit because you're paying someone last minute and all the decor and food will probably have to be purchased instead of made. Or maybe you're tasked with the family reunion, but you've planned enough small parties and dinners that you live in fear of the little things you'll forget that will turn the event into a disaster.

Let us help - we can plan the actual event, sure, but better yet? Let us teach you how to do it. We'll give you timelines and ideas, guidelines to get it done little by little in six months or at a dizzying pace in two weeks because you just found this book and the calendar snuck up on you.

Either way, we've got you covered, and your small event will be a flawless success - whether this book turns you into the neighborhood or family go-to planner, a confident home party guru, or even a professional, is entirely up to you!

Chapter 1

Types of "small" events

First, what counts as a "small event"? There's a general standard that if your event hosts less than one hundred people, it falls into the small event category. But like most everything in life, that's not always the exact standard. I got the event-planning bug from my aunt, and she's so kind as to let the family professional help but not take over - and I thank you, Aunt Jane, because you guys don't pay me!

But Aunt Jane can flawlessly and effortlessly host 150-200 guests a couple of times a year, that's how good she is. A big house and a big yard with a family who knows the annual reunion and the occasional milestone birthday or anniversary party will be at her house, and everything is down to a routine. Two hundred guests make for a small event with Aunt Jane and I running the show - but I'm a pro and Aunt Jane is retired with 40 years' experience running the same show at the same place with the same guests.

That doesn't mean though that you should feel like a failure if the 50 person guest list for your daughter's backyard wedding - while your family members all juggle 40-plus hour work weeks and children, different time zones, travel budget constraints, vacation times, and life responsibilities - makes you feel a little frazzled and you're starting to consider slipping her a couple of thousand bucks to elope to Vegas.

So an event being "small" or "completely out my range of sanity" is going to vary depending on your experience, schedule, and quite a few other constraints that may change all the time, but the rule of a thumb is that a guest list of over 100 starts to be a larger event.

Here are a few events that fall into the category of small events, again depending on guest list size:

A family birthday party

Most family birthday parties aren't going to reach a guest list of 100 people unless Grandma is hitting the centenarian mark and the family is flying in from all over the country to celebrate her amazing life. Those parties happen, and they're great - a rare opportunity to listen to Uncle Jimmy's rants about the Democrats and taxes when there isn't a giant stuffed turkey waiting to be eaten on the table. Your sister's 26th birthday dinner or Mom's 50th though are lovely but simpler affairs - siblings, parents, grandparents, the children, and maybe a couple of the closest friends and some significant others. With a large family this might be 40 people; with a small one having an intimate gathering of the closest members, maybe 10 or 15 people.

A child's birthday party

Children's parties, as we all know, are bigger events than adult birthday parties. Children are still excited about getting older and aren't endangering the house when the candles are put on the cake. They like to play and run. You'll need an appropriate location and a lot of patience for all the children you'll be inviting, and you'll have to decide on your sanity and the budget versus the unwavering love for your baby while you determine if the guest list will include his or her entire class or just the neighbors.

A family vacation

This counts as a small event, and if you've ever tried to plan one that wasn't just "lay on the beach and don't move," you know it can be quite an experience! You may only have five people or less in tow, but you have to get everyone there with all the right things packed, you have to hit all the sites without missing anything, you want a hotel that won't require disinfectant, and you need to do it all without breaking the bank or your sanity. An event planner can handle all of this for you - or we can show you how to do a lot of it!

An anniversary dinner

Here is a truly special event - most of the time an anniversary dinner is just going to be a special date night for a couple, if even that when the kids are young and the focus isn't on the pair for a few years (or decades). But a silver or golden anniversary requires a celebration! Not too many blessed unions make it that far and there's a family full of loved ones who want to celebrate with the couple. So if your parents - or you, or anyone close to you - is coming up on a milestone anniversary, plan an event to show your love and gratitude!

The annual holiday get-together

So this one happens every year, and it's at the same time and the same place and everyone brings the same plate, right? Well, maybe. But even that's more difficult to coordinate than you realize if you aren't the one hosting, and then of course circumstances change. Has Thanksgiving always been held at Mom's house, but there's a remodel going on or Dad's medical treatment means he needs a quiet house? Is it the first year all the kids are living away from home or they're rotating the holidays with their spouse's family? The kid at college is going through a vegan phase and bringing home the hippie boyfriend with a gluten allergy to meet the conservative Republican family? You see, it's harder than you think! You'll need a seating chart this year - he can't sit next to Uncle Bill with the hunting stories or Cousin Nancy who trolls socialists on Facebook.

An office party

Office parties are a lot of fun - a rare chance for coworkers to let their hair down together instead of stress over deadlines and crises. They have to be planned pretty far in advance though, especially holiday parties, or you get stuck with the only opening being the last week in November or the week after Christmas at a local greasy spoon. And you have to consider your staff as well - anyone who can't do certain days or hours, who doesn't drink or has sensitive allergies?

The work retreat

This is a fun one but it's pretty complicated! Do you want to plan a fun family day at the office or do you want staff to get away together for team building over a weekend? Either way, you have to consider their other obligations - second jobs, caregiver schedules, and so on - and you have to plan activities they can all do together. The biggest thing to look out for here is to make sure everyone feels included - don't plan a ropes course if you have a staff member in a wheelchair and don't plan it over a major religious holiday that only one or a couple members of your team celebrate.

A reunion

Family reunions are a favorite, but they're stressful! The same complications arise here - which branch of the family and how far up? When can they all travel? How many people are there? Is there a way to include those who definitely can't come? How will you entertain so many people all day?

A block party

Basically, a block party is a reunion but for neighbors, not family. You don't have to take as many factors into consideration - everyone is close by, definitely! And availability might not be as important; if it lasts all day, just about everyone can swing by for a few minutes. You just have to make it fun, feed the people well, and be very careful to make sure everyone knows about it and feels welcome in the space.

Church or class events

These can be monsters! You have a guest list pretty much built-in but you have schedules to consider and everyone's needs to meet. What will everyone who attends enjoy? If you don't know everyone, how can you make sure everyone is included?

While the recap of what qualifies as a small event is pretty basic, keep in mind it's going to vary for everyone. If you're exceptionally busy with five kids and a forty-hour workweek on top of church and volunteer groups and an active family, you'll find a family dinner for 10 harder to coordinate than Aunt Jane's 200 person holiday get-togethers. The key is planning - if you're too busy, we get it! Plan far in advance, so that you only need a few minutes here and there and can spend weeks not even thinking about it but still keep it under control. If you have less on your plate, you can handle a bigger event with fewer heads-up.

Chapter 2

The pre-planning planning

Not every event planner is going to tell you to do this, but for me, it's essential: you need to pregame your event. Depending on how organized you are and how invested you are in it, you could create a scrapbook or a Pinterest board with all the ideas you'd love to implement. Create your dream event - at dream level, it doesn't even have to be a "small" event. For your wildest fantasy throwdown, you can invite the entire city and serve gold-leaf foie gras, fly in Beyonce to perform and hire flying ponies.

That's step one, and it's the fun part. A few steps later comes the harder part when you admit to yourself that ponies can't fly, you don't even like foie gras, and Beyonce blocked your calls. But for now, have fun with your ideas, because when you are dreaming big that's when you really are looking at everything out there and you find ideas that really get you excited about the event - you were just going to throw Grandma an 80th birthday party with a sheet cake from the grocery store and a half-hearted triple round chorus of Happy Birthday with the grandkids, but you didn't even know wheelchair relay races could be so much fun - and maybe you can find that long-lost World War II-era first love she still gets misty-eyed over! That couldn't go wrong and it looked so sweet in that Lifetime movie.

Once you've dreamed big, start narrowing it down. First, start working on the real guest list. This is not finalized yet; it can still be way too long and include some random person you met on the subway six months that made you laugh and you think would be a real hoot at the party. Then, pick a date - don't check Beyonce's tour schedule; deep down you know that idea is getting the ax in a little while. Take out your calendar and pick a few dates that definitely work for you, and then start considering the people on the invite list. If you definitely want to invite the Collinses but you know that's their anniversary weekend, either change the date or move the Collinses to another list - by the way, you're going to make two lists: an "invite/definitely hope they'll attend" list, and an "invite/they probably won't come but it would be rude not to make the gesture" list.

Why would you do that? Well, it affects friendships to not be invited. I'll give you an example - I'm an event planner! And I travel quite often. With that combination, I am frequently invited to events that I can't personally attend. Some people send me an invitation and know that I'm probably not going to make it - and it warms my heart to be remembered. I go when I can, and if I can't, I'll usually send something along - if not a gift delivered with a friend attending, then a floral arrangement or donation for a fundraiser or something of the sort. But I also have friends who just say "She's never there, I'm not wasting an invitation on her." And even though rationally I understand that, and I'm an event planner so I shouldn't be offended at the logic, it still bothers me when I find out everyone is going to attend a party I didn't even know was going to happen until last minute. Imagine your friends who aren't event planners and don't have that understanding - they'll take it personally. Waste the few invites on people you know won't make it just so you don't hurt feelings of people you care about.

But back to the date - at this point, you're working on the guest list and date simultaneously, and as far as you know, Beyonce might still be able to make it. Once you've decided that the dates you are working with so far are okay to your knowledge with everyone on the list - and this is just preliminary; you can't possibly know everyone's anniversary and birthday, vacation time, and sister's wedding date - make sure the date doesn't conflict with anything else. It might be a religious holiday or a big town festival; if half the guest list is faculty at the local university, you might not want to plan a fall festival over Homecoming weekend or a spring fling during finals week or graduation.

Choose no more than three potential dates and put them in order of preference, then do a poll with close friends or family to see if they know of any conflicts with those dates. Consider the significance of the conflicts before you rule a date out - if the Democratic National Convention is being held that weekend in your city, it might not affect you if you only associate with Republicans, but it will no matter what if you only live half a mile from the convention center - you might not want to change the event date but you'll at least want to look into other locations.

Alter your choices as needed and settle on your final date. Now you need to set your budget realistically. This is the part that's going to break your heart a little bit - Beyonce probably won't be able to make it if your budget is below six figures, and I know it's tough but you'll probably have to cancel the laser lights show and tone down the menu. How we choose what we can do with what we have to work with will come later. If you have serious budget constraints, the best thing you can do is plan far ahead - if you can only do $500 for a party, it's probably going to be tight, but if you're working on it six months ahead, $84 a month might make it seem like less of a stretch. If you analyze your personal expenditures, you might even say "Okay, maybe I can double it" and the party becomes a lot easier, just because you realized you can skip a couple of meals out every month or hit the coffee shop every other day instead of every day, a little more Metro and a little less Uber.

But what if you step out of the fantasy world planning stages and realize your budget is actually zero? This is actually a very realistic scenario, and don't feel bad about it. Your little girl deserves a first birthday party and you want the memories, but you're a single mom behind on the rent, maybe. Most of us have had this situation, maybe not with the same causes but the same end result, and it's part of life. All the more to plan ahead - you can throw the party of the year on a budget, and if you're working six months ahead, you can call in the grandparents, aunts, and uncles, and godparents or your best friends to pitch in a little. Grab a few of them, explain the situation, give them the plan you'll have put together by the time you finish this book, and ask them to pitch in $25 a month or something of the sort, so that by party day you have maybe as much as $1000, and none of you felt the effects of handing over such a big chunk of change.

So right now, you're still in the pregaming stage - the last time you seriously considered how the party would look, you were considering a $3,000,000 budget. You're leaving that alone for now but you know, as crushing as it is, the gift bags from Tiffany's and Gucci probably won't happen. You've got your party date and you have a budget in mind. The further out you plan this event, the more impressive you can make a small budget look. For now you can still have your giant guest list, but go ahead and accept now that if your budget is looking like $5 per person, you should probably get used to the idea that you'll need to cut out the UPS driver, your son's cafeteria ladies, and the lifeguard at the Y. Even though you don't need to cut anyone yet, get a solid number in your head of how many to invite.

Chapter 3

Vendors vs Doing it Yourself

You found everything you need on Pinterest; you don't need to buy anything - you tell yourself before you do the math and realize what you have planned will cost you approximately 200 man-hours and the equivalent of the outstanding balance on your student loans at the craft store.

Here's a tip that's more of a lifestyle change, and hear me out before "On this episode of Hoarders..." starts playing in your head. Start saving everything - cereal boxes, egg cartons, soda bottles, plastic bags, shoe boxes, cardboard, and packing supplies, and anything else that you can imagine would come in handy and you see frequently listed in do-it-yourself crafting tutorials. Collect the tools and crafts you find on sale. I am not a crafter; I lose patience and interest 30 seconds in and all I've done is cut about two inches into a piece of construction paper before I'm frantically searching for someone to delegate to.

But I'm a mom and I'm a party planner, and sometimes I have twelve hours or no budget and have to turn a pumpkin into a coach. Now, I have to let you know, I am a neat freak and a minimalist when it comes to "stuff" - just the idea of collecting things makes my heart race. So we aren't talking a hoarder's nest, free for all, rodent attracting trash dump. Don't bring in this trash to treasure unless you're able to immediately put it away and condense it as much as possible. For example, those egg cartons stack (and make great dividers for other projects) and cereal boxes flatten. You've got to hide it away and keep it clean and organized.

If you can do this, you can DIY just about anything. If you can't keep it clean, don't try it, and plan those crafts far in advance, begging the supplies off neighbors, friends, and family, and suffering the $10,000 shopping run to the craft store. It's a choice.

If you plan to DIY your event, depending on the event type it can be extremely easy or it can be far beyond your capabilities, and you need to identify that before getting too far into the party planning, or you'll lose control and be in over your head before you even really begin. Obviously, DIY isn't much of a factor if you're talking about a family vacation or getting everyone together for a family dinner in a restaurant. You can make t-shirts and pins and an event hashtag for Instagram if you really want to, but your occasion won't be lacking without it. There are levels to this - DIY typically means you're going to make your own centerpieces, not handblow the glass and design the candles.

On the other hand, I have on multiple occasions absolutely had brides custom design and make candles, and I've had custom-designed glass at a wedding too - the father of the groom was a professional glassblower and craftsman. The bride wore a custom handcrafted gown too; her best friend was a costume designer. In context, it wasn't insane at all; what might sound like a bridezilla who lost all control of her mental faculties was, in fact, a joyous occasion full of thoughtful and gorgeous personal touches, and was completely within their means. And that's the point here; stay within your means with the crafting goals.

Do it yourself isn't just about decor though; we're talking about food and activities too. I tend to be pro-caterer but also lean towards doing it yourself for games and activities, but I'll be forthcoming with the pros and cons of both.

Decor

In my mind, whether you're DIYing the decor, or buying or renting premade should depend, not just on budget and time (and skill, if we're being honest), but also on the event itself. If you're doing a sophisticated event, like a very elegant wedding, consider a vendor. Now, since we're mostly talking about small events, you're probably planning a laid-back simple backyard wedding. Nothing wrong with DIY here - in fact even some of the most elegant, memorable, or beautiful weddings I've seen have been do-it-yourself - this is about resources and creativity, and quite simply, whether you have the time or want to put much time into it.

See the appendix for a checklist on decor items you won't want to forget in order to keep your event from looking bare. You'll want to consider your tables and chairs - centerpieces and tablecloths and runners, and chair covers. The lighting and candles, flowers, balloons, banners, and streamers, along with any other wall decor should be considered. Decorate doors and ceilings at the minimum, and adorn tables with centerpieces. Anything beyond that can be at your discretion depending on funds and style preferences.

Food

When it comes to food, I generally lean pro-caterer or restaurant service, and here's why: it's a lot of work and people get overwhelmed. The food is still being set out when people arrive, half gets forgotten, and it gets served cold. And of course, there's a hot mess to clean up later. Food will actually be discussed in more detail in a later chapter, but you should consider the resources of time and storage - plus you may have to consider prep - if your budget is low so you assume you'll be cooking, make sure you have the proper tools or you can borrow to prepare the food - it would be very easy to rack up $1000 just in pots and pans before you even buy the food.

And honestly, it isn't always cheaper to buy your own food. Caterers get bulk discounts on food items, and you might have to buy a bag of flour to just use a cup. Keep all this in mind. Consider a caterer for your event - it may end up better, faster, easier, and believe it or not, cheaper!

Activities

When it comes to the activities for your party, this is another one that depends on your budget and time, and maybe even your personality. I'm a big fan of bouncy castles and Slip 'n Slides, and those are clearly vendor-supplies items. A circulating face painter and balloon animal artist in between the Disney princesses and circus-trained dogs is also enjoyable, albeit impractical for most small events.

But just a few minutes on Pinterest will spark enough ideas you'll need to expand the party into the neighbor's backyard. One of my favorites is a Twister board painted directly onto the grass, and you can set up food fight and water stations, relays, and games using simple household items and just a little arts and crafts and set-up time.

Start checking out local party rental vendors and caterers to see what they offer and what their price range is. Once you have an idea of how that fits into your budget, you'll know if vendors are an option or you'll need to plan ahead for a more creative but hands-on do it yourself experience. It's good to have those resources saved anyway because you'll have a jump start on any other events you plan in the future.

So you have a budget of $1000, a guest list of 200, the bouncy castle and fire juggler together will be $600, but you have to purchase insurance and they have to be located three football fields away from one another because the castle is flammable. The caterer is going to charge $10 per cake slice and that's after you took off the edible gold leafing.

Hold that thought - you're going to reanalyze all of that in a few minutes. Your dream event is not going to feature Beyonce performing in a bouncy castle but you'll find yourself just as happy in the end, even with all your compromises.

Chapter 4

Location

One of the biggest factors in your party planning will be location. Most small events are held in a backyard or a house, but if you're getting close to that 100 person level-up, or you're just not into home entertainment, there are plenty of options to consider.

If you're the planner and this is a gathering of people you know well, your own home is your best option. But you need to be realistic too. My house doesn't work; I live thirty minutes outside of town. It's especially bad for a kid's party, lacking a landscaped lawn and full of trees, close to cliffs and streams that are a danger to young guests.

Are you centrally located? Do you have plenty of space and lots of bathrooms? Are you a decent housekeeper? House in good shape?

You know what makes your home a good or a bad candidate better than I. If your spouse is chronically ill and can't handle disruptions, if you have any particular personal drama going on, a house remodel, or a ghost who likes to torment little girls with braids or men who pull for the New England Patriots, consider another location.

On the plus side, it's free and you know your schedule, where to hide the dirty laundry, and what you can cook in your own kitchen. If you fall behind on prep, you can decorate at 2:00 in the morning and you don't have to figure out how to transport the entire menu for 85 people, along with all the decor and your family.

I mentioned that my house would never work, but my father's house, centrally located with a big yard and a lot of parking – it most definitely would, if it was a thirty person guest list. His house is cozy. But he's dealing with a lot of illness so we'd have to plan carefully around his day and keep people out of the back where his bedroom is. If our guest list were approaching 100, my grandparents' farm would be perfect. But no one lives there anymore and every family get-together requires a deep clean just because of the dust. Again, it's all going to come down to resources, and the pros and cons for each location will vary widely depending on various factors including event type and guest list. Consider who you know who would be willing to offer up their spaces.

If your house won't cut it for your event and no one else has better options, time to look into other local resources. Consider your budget, space, and time of year first. Local parks are usually very affordably priced – and for anything more than a handful of people you'll want to reserve a space, especially if needing a staging area, but if your event is in December when it snows or it's – for example – an April wedding and the bride has severe hay fever, you may want an indoor location.

Local churches usually have facilities that can host a small event easily – and they're usually inexpensive too. Bonus points if you're a member of the church; you might get the space free or close to it (as in as low as $20). My suggestion though is that you add to it in appreciation for the church's generosity. I donate to make a total of at least $100 and/or double the asking fee, whichever is greater unless the church has rented the space to me at a rate close to or on par with standard rentals in my area – most churches are great economical spaces, but some are in high demand and price accordingly.

Civic spaces are usually more economical as well, though not on the same scale as local churches, and their fees skyrocket faster depending on the demand. They're generally, if you choose an outdoor space anyway, very picturesque and family-friendly gathering spaces (indoors could be hit or miss).

Your next option is a private space – a banquet hall or local business that provides rooms or open areas for private celebrations. For children's parties, you might be thinking of anything from Chuck E. Cheese Pizza or a water park to a children's museum or local farm that's open to the public. For other parties, maybe we're talking about private gardens, an art museum, or just a local hall. It depends on the local resources. The benefit to many of these, though it will vary widely, is that they may provide set-up and clean-up or offer vendors for equipment rental and catering. Public spaces usually don't, but that varies widely too. The services the place provides will be reflected in pricing, so keep that in mind while seeking options for the event.

If your budget extends into space rental you have many, many options. But you'll have to remember that you lose a little more control (while also gaining some more help). The private spaces can range from no cost if the food is included to thousands of dollars, so the sky is really the limit here. You may have to live with rules as to what activities you can plan, what food to bring in, hours, sound ordinances, parking access, décor, and so on.

At your own home, you can host a 3-day electronic music festival with a full barbecue pit for your one-year-old's first birthday party, if you really want to and you grease the hands of your homeowner's association to forget the sound ordinance for a little while. But if you choose the local vegan hippie commune because of the amazing views, they won't let you roast a pig on a spit and the music festival is likely out too.

Once you have the budget and date determined, you'll want to decide quickly on your location too. These factors will steer a lot of the rest of your planning, but if you have your heart set on a real hot spot, they book fast. I have planned weddings at places that book two years in advance, and I have planned birthday parties that I had to throw together last minute and could only find sites that required a lot of flexibility, compromise, and improvisation.

Also consider flexibility with dates until you have your perfect location – if you narrow your date down to three choices and the space of your dreams is available on the third of those, you have to decide if the date or the place is more important. In my experience, the date is the one that gets the boot, but that is not always the case. Every planner has a different set of priorities.

Chapter 5

Guestlist and invitations

Your guest list is going to be one of the most stressful parts of event planning but can be easy to work around. You have probably finished up a dream list, but now it's time to be realistic. Your whole town can't come when you have a budget to worry about! You will need to plan for your budget, space, and any internal wars that may be going on with attendees. On top of that, you will need to consider your invites' appearance and form, and understand a few of your guests will bring along their own guests as well.

As mentioned, your dream guest list may very well not be in your budget. Some of your guests are likely to bring extra people with them, but this doesn't exactly mean there will be too many attendees - only about 70-80% of invited people are going to come, so their guests will fill in the blank spots.

When you start narrowing down your list, do it in tiers. Your closest friends and family get first priority, and if the budget or space is very constricted but you have a large network, you might even limit that. Once you've considered your closest and dearest, review potential guests in groups - coworkers, neighbors, church family, and so on. I usually invite neighbors or coworkers above all else and then expand outward to church members, less close friends, and family, colleagues from volunteer events, and miscellaneous contacts picked up over the years. Your priority system may vary according to the event - I might cast a fairly wide net for my wedding if I have a big budget and small network, but if my budget for my baby's first birthday party is limited, don't invite people outside your immediate circle who don't have small children.

If there happen to be any possible guests with extreme feuds but the location will be small, you might want to consider not inviting at least one of them. However, you don't want to find yourself accidentally in the feud or showing favorites; if you have a larger location, you can address this issue in a different way, inviting both guests and allowing them to avoid one another.

When you consider your guest list, your budget will be one of the main factors in your decision. You will need to consider the invites you send, if you send any at all, as a nice invitation can cost up to ten dollars each.

When we think of an invitation to an event, we think of a letter or card. For many events, this is still exactly the case but others may need only a Facebook page event invite or even just word of mouth. Before creating or buying your invites, consider if a physical one is even needed. If you opt for it, you have plenty more to consider.

The decision to purchase invitations will depend on what your event is for. A child's birthday will need a card, but a small office party won't. There is a middle ground between these two options though, and in that situation, you may want to consider electronic invites. This form of invite is generally free and can be done through a variety of websites that will send the invite through an email, or you can create a Facebook event page and invite people through the share and invite functions. But you don't want strangers to see details about the event, you can make a connected Facebook group and add people there. Electronic invitations are great for anyone who wants to cut down on paper and fuel usage or to invite out of country or otherwise long-distance people to the event. On top of that, it frees up your budget to splurge in other areas.

Invitations are the first truly official sneak peeks of your event that others will see. They are almost like an advertisement of information to draw in a crowd. For some businesses, this invite really is a sort of advertisement and they will need just the right invitations to get started. While you may have chosen electronic methods, a physical invitation can add a personal touch to any important attendees and send the message that the potential attendee is truly wanted. The right invitation will depend on the theme and tone of your event, so choose carefully!

If your event has a particular theme and tone, your invitation should be a taste of it, giving the invitee an idea of formality, and perhaps for children an idea for gifts. (Paw Patrol theme? This kid loves dogs.) This is probably the most important factor in invitation choice - setting the tone. You won't be choosing a child's race car themed birthday card for invitations to a formal and expensive black-tie affair wedding, for example.

To match your event be aware of the details such as color schemes, topic or purpose, date and time, and so on, to really design the best invitation. While fitting invitations may be found in card stores, you may not be able to purchase enough for your event without placing a custom order that takes time to receive.

Ordering online will likely be the best option, and they should include several customization options. With some sites, you may be able to design the invitation yourself. You can design up or down based on the budget you've designed, and bear in mind that per piece prices tend to go down when ordering in large quantities. The quantities for price drop will vary from store to store, but most would require a bulk purchase of 100 - out of the scope of planning small events. While pricing, make sure you take into account postage - both to reach you, as bulk paper gets heavy, and to mail out individually.

Again, the right time to send out invitations will depend on your event, the people you're inviting, and your type of invitation - if it needs time to travel in the post, where it is going, how much RSVP time is needed, and so on. Also, consider the time of year it is and if you will need to expect post to take longer due to holidays, weather, and so on.

What should you include on your invitation? This might depend on the event, but there are standards to this that reach across all types. Obviously, a date and time with the name and address of the location are absolutely necessary. You'll want to let people know what type of event it is (birthday party, anniversary, wedding, et cetera) and who the honored person is, the dress code suggestion or requirements, and response guidelines as necessary and appropriate. Depending on formality and your amount of time and organization, it's a good idea to include the invited attendees' names on the card itself, but that is often cost-prohibitive on bulk purchase cards rather than the cheaper, fill in the blank versions.

Once you have your guest list and you've sent out invitations, as the responses come in you can begin planning the seating charts. Not every event will need one, but it's likely that a more formal event such as a wedding will require one. These help avoid confusion, keep people organized, and prevent possible altercations between members - and thinking more positively - help like-minded people enjoy your event and establish new contacts and relationships.

Before fully charting out the seating arrangements, be sure to check over who is invited and have confirmed their attendance. Families will prefer to sit together, and with any people they have brought as their plus-ones as well. If there is space you may want to consider smaller details, such as the mother with a small child who may want to sit near the back and near an exit or open area in case a break is needed - truthfully, that might be in the event's best interest too.

Of course, be sure to not sit anyone who dislikes another too close if possible. Many a family feud has stolen the spotlight from a bride and groom when wide berth isn't given between warring factions. In the event of a wedding, it's expected the couple's families are near the front. Put these notes in a clear list for reference.

How much space does your location have? The amount of area will heavily affect your seating chart, and you will want to be aware of the space's layout. No one wants to be away from easy access to exits, the dance floor, serving tables, or other amenities, but elderly people or young children, anyone ill, and so on, will appreciate their needs being met and being placed closer to some areas for better access.

Use our guides in the appendix to help with your guest list and seating charts.

Chapter 6

Food

When planning the menu for your event, you need to consider many factors: budget, theme, whether or not you would like to have an outside caterer handle the food, as well as what the primary focus of the event is going to be. For example, a family reunion is going to revolve around eating whereas a children's birthday party is going to be heavily focused on games and entertainment, with a birthday cake potentially being the only food item served. For a wedding reception, you may decide that alcohol and the wedding cake are where the bulk of your food budget is going to be spent if you decide to offer an open bar.

But whatever you decide, you need to know the exact amount you are willing to spend or you can easily blow your entire event budget on just food and drinks.

Once you are sure about how much money you're allotting for food, it is a good idea to call a few catering companies in your area and get prices from them. Most people think of catered events as having hired wait staff the company sends along to serve, in addition to them preparing the food and setting up the food and drink tables.

If you hire a caterer for their full services they will generally provide their own linens and tables, will set up and clean up and even put up your decorations for you. They can provide plates, cups, cutlery, champagne flutes, and essentially anything else last-minute your event. Essentially, a caterer is more than happy to provide any service you desire, keeping in mind that they will charge for each service they do for you.

However, it is not necessary to hire a caterer for all of the services they provide and sometimes it is cheaper to use them for some things than for you to do it yourself. Not to mention, the reduced workload, prep, and not having to stress over-preparing, cooking, and storing the food in your own kitchen may well be worth the money for you.

Catering companies generally have several different options that are at different price points, as well as several different types of menus they can design around your personal food preferences and/or food allergy considerations. Prices are usually given in cost per person, but again, anything can be negotiated with a caterer - you may just have to cut out some of their services in order to stay within your budget.

If you are fine with decorating and setting up yourself, you have your own linens and dinnerware, and you just want them to cook for you, they have serving platters called chafers with warmers called sternos underneath that once lit, keep the food hot for 4-6 hours. In addition, if all you want to do is rent their linens and chafing dishes, many companies will let you do that too - so you can keep the food you cook yourself hot (or cold depending on the dish) without having to make a significant investment in equipment you'll never use again.

You might be surprised how cheaply caterers are willing to do some or all of these things; again, it all depends on how much of a focus the food and alcohol will be at your event, as well as the time and personal kitchen space you have available to devote to the food for your event.

If you decide to handle the food and drinks yourself, there are tricks that can save you time and money as well as a few simple rules of thumb to keep in mind so that you don't wind up with a ton of leftovers, or even worse, without enough food and a bunch of hungry guests who came expecting to be fed.

Depending on the size of your guest list you may have all the dinnerware you need for everyone; just keep in mind if you serve yourself and you serve using non-disposable dinnerware of your own, you will have a lot of dishes to do at the end of the evening. Party supply stores are great places to find nice disposable plates, cutlery, glasses, champagne flutes, and other items at very reasonable prices.

This will keep you from having a lot of clean up at the end and will also keep your guests from returning to the food table multiple times with the same dish, which could possibly cause food contamination (an important consideration if any of your guests have food allergies). These days there are also many options for table covers and linens that look much nicer than the cheap plastic tablecloths that tear the minute anyone touches them and used to be the only option for disposable linens. Another possibility to consider when deciding about linens and dinnerware, if the event you are hosting is a family reunion, is to ask another family member to handle that part of the food portion of the event.

Family reunions can be handled slightly different than other events because all the guests are family - but the notion of asking a guest to handle part of the food isn't limited strictly to reunions. For example, it would not be improper etiquette when planning your child's first birthday to ask the godmother to provide the cake.

In fact, people often appreciate being asked to be involved in the party planning because it lets them know that you consider them to have a closer relationship with you than other guests, and people like feeling needed. As long as it is someone you can trust to complete the task, then that alleviates one more stress and takes a to-do item off of your personal plate.

If you've decided to do all of the cooking and food presentations yourself, you should plan a menu with items that you can cook and store before the day of the event, as you will not have time to get all the cooking done that morning. Plus, if you procrastinate to cook on the day of the event, Murphy's law will likely come visit you and something will go wrong, and you won't have time to cook things over again that day.

If you buy a cake from a bakery, the number of people they say it will serve should be accurate. But if you are baking at home from a box, you should assume it will serve half as many people as it says it does. When serving bite-size appetizers, you should make enough for every guest to have three of each appetizer.

Once you put the food out on the presentation table you should label every item - and on the label, list any ingredient you used which is a common allergen. If this event is large enough that you send out RSVP, there should be a place on there for people to list any allergies they have and you should take that into consideration so that you don't cook any allergen-free food in the same cookware that you cook the rest of the menu in. A good host should always have some item that people with allergies can feel free to eat and should not put that food out on the same table with the rest so that people without allergies don't eat it all and leave nothing for the guests who can't eat the other food options.

When it comes to alcohol, you need to consider how much you can spend on alcohol, because as much as you are willing to provide your guests, they will drink. Doing a full open bar can be one of the most expensive components of a wedding reception. It is not necessary to provide your guests with an unlimited supply of alcoholic beverages.

One tip that people have found helpful is to give every guest a certain number of tickets when they arrive, for example, 3. They can turn each ticket in for one free drink, and after they have used all their tickets they can continue to get drinks, but it would be a cash bar. This idea works best if you have someone serving as a bartender for the event, but this person does not have to be a hired bartender, though many people choose to do that. This is another job you can give to one of the "guests" who is more like family: godfather, grandfather, uncle, etc.

Keep the options limited so that you can buy in bulk and save money. And remember, if you are not comfortable with a lot of guests at your event drinking heavily, or at all, that is completely acceptable. This is an event you are planning, not them. If someone feels alcohol is necessary at an event, they can host their own!

The goal in event planning is to create memories that your guests will enjoy and that you will too. By preparing everything in advance, sticking to your budget, utilizing close friends and family to help, and making calls to see how a caterer can help provide you with the things you may not have at home or be able to do on your own, you will be free to enjoy yourself on the day of the event and be present in the moment for whatever occasion you've worked so hard to create a memorable day for.

Chapter 7

Entertainment

It is important that you plan your entertainment for any event in advance with consideration for the age of participants, budget, and time of year, day of the week, location, safety, reliability, and food availability. Some entertainment is relevant for all special events but can be sourced through friends and family so that money can be spent on other entertainment which requires more specialization.

Having a photographer for events is almost always encouraged; however, it may not be a situation where you need to pay for someone to come to the event. You will need to find someone though who will commit to being the party photographer. You may have the perfect person in your family or friends invite list.

Music can be as simple as setting up a Bluetooth speaker and finding a channel appropriate to the guest of honor or theme. For a more personalized or special touch, a live band can really create the wow factor you are looking for.

Take into account the differences between event types:

Vacation

When planning your vacation it is relatively easy to find entertainment within the city or in local communities. Planning your outings to events can and should be done in advance of your vacation. If you are staying in a hotel or resort, those resorts have all the contacts you need for reliable businesses that are prepared to enrich your vacation time with fun, exciting or romantic entertainment. The resorts and hotel may also be able to schedule and reserve event slots for you. Make sure to plan events around times when you believe all of the guests will be available - although you don't want to fill your days with too many events because you don't want to overwhelm yourself.

One to two events per day is appropriate and will allow time for relaxation. For example, if you have a free day, schedule outdoor events during the day with time between to relax before the next event. Perhaps a trip to a local nature reserve during the day with a break for napping and relaxing before a dinner theatre experience will be just right.

In tourist communities, there will be opportunities for events generally on high traffic streets and alleyways. Caricature artists and street performers will be plentiful as well as musicians. If you haven't scheduled events and just want to explore, street performers usually set up in high pedestrian traffic areas and will be easy to find. If you aren't familiar with the area, the hotels and resorts can let you know if those areas are within walking distance and in many cases can provide transportation for you.

Don't forget to budget for your events so that you get the most entertainment for your money. Take into account the age range of the vacationing parties so that there won't be people you are dragging through events in which they are disinterested.

Birthday

Birthday events are unique and need specialized entertainment which is cohesive to the theme of the party and centered around the likes and dislikes of the guest of honor. Entertainment really depends on the age of the birthday person. For example, a 10-year-old boy may be more interested in magicians, petting zoos or clowns. If a party has a theme centered on cars, you may want to visit a race track or local car show. A grown woman's' birthday may be more suited to karaoke, DJ or a band. It too would need to be centered on the theme of the event.

An older woman may want a less intense entertainment than a younger woman. This is an opportunity to take into account the personality, likes and dislikes of the guest of honor for which the party is being thrown. Some kids have aversions to masked, costumed entertainment. If you're not part of the family and unfamiliar with the birthday girl or boy, it may be wise to check with the parents.

Anniversary

Anniversary entertainment is much like birthday events in that you want to make sure that the entertainment is specialized to the couple who is celebrating their anniversary. Entertainment that really is centered on things that they as a couple enjoy or focuses on them is important. Some ideas that may be appropriate would include concerts, musicians, and videographers for the memorable moments and definitely a scheduled photographer. The videographer and or photographer doesn't necessarily have to be someone who is a professional but needs to be someone who is reliable and available for the event. For a super memorable event, you will want to take a visual record of who attended and special messages to the couple and videographers and photographers can do that easily.

Holiday party

Most holiday parties are themed and need entertainment to be specialized and cohesive as well. An Easter party may not need music but a Christmas party most definitely will so take the type of holiday you are preparing for into account. Photographers are always needed for special events like holiday parties which happen only once a year.

Weddings

Weddings can be some of the most special events in a person's lifetime, so it is very important to create the type of environment that will be the most memorable. Receptions can be very expensive, so make sure that you are budgeting funds on the most important things to the cohesiveness of the event and resourcing entertainment appropriately. There are many types of entertainment appropriate for a wedding. Wedding singers, karaoke, DJs, bands, photographers, videographers, ice carvers, etc. For a more personal touch make sure that DJs and singers have the couple's favorite songs in different genres, making sure to have beautiful romantic moments planned as well as festive party favorites. For the most special occasion, a live band can be the most personal touch.

Vacations, birthdays, receptions and parties all have varying atmospheres and experiences as the goal; specialized entertainment can make the difference between a ho-hum activity and the get-together of a lifetime.

Chapter 8

Decor

The decorations for your event are almost as important as the event itself. Decorations help set the theme and tone while bringing the attendees closer to the meaning behind the event. Depending on your theme and cause, decorations can be very simple. Many events will only need a few table pieces, some tablecloths, simple balloons, and maybe some banners. However, not all events are the same, and there are a few things you will want to plan out before even searching for your decorations. Setting up your decorations can be an issue depending on the space and layout of your area, but will change the whole mood of the event to something even better. A good setup of decorations makes everything flow together and prevents overcrowding and heightens the story.

Planning

Before looking for your decorations, you need to consider the demographic and theme of the event. A superhero birthday party is going to have different decorations than a 50th-anniversary dinner. Of course, you should also consider your budget. Your decorations will also depend on the space you are planning for, such as indoors versus outdoors, how much square footage and the furniture you have, and if there are any guidelines in the venue you are using.

Indoors

An indoor event will not generally need waterproof items, and using paper or tassels will not be much of a problem. While there is less room to spread out, there is more room to decorate due to walls, ceilings, and doorways.

If you are setting up for a small indoor area you should not have many decorations that will sit on the floor, as they take up useful walking space. You can have a few here and there, right next to doors (without blocking them) or to fill in spaces no one would need to use as-is. A larger indoor space though will be able to fit more, and floor decorations can be tasteful to sort and guide the area.

Outdoors

Decorating an outdoor event can sometimes be harder if there is no shelter, as most decorations will go onto tables, chairs, and onto the lawn. Lawn decorations will usually be statues or other figures. All decorations will need to be windproof, and preferably waterproof. If you are renting a space from a popular venue, it is likely that the outdoor space will already have "natural" decoration, such as being a beautiful garden. In this case, you will probably not want much more decoration other than enough to make it relevant to your event. Be sure to ask the venue if there are certain decorations to be avoided, such as anything with fumes that may harm the area.

A small outdoor area tends to be very easy to decorate, depending on your location. For a backyard, you can decorate the fences or trees and add in posts to decorate with arches or signs. Parks can be a little difficult and will have some guidelines you need to follow, which will affect the types of decorations you're going to put up. A larger outdoor area is likely going to be a venue, and have some sort of flora already around.

5 Easy Steps

●   Consider the theme - what decorations go into this usually and in what colors?

●   Search other events with this theme, and gain ideas from there

●   Add in your budget, and consider which decorations will take more funds than others (for example, fresh flowers will be more expensive than balloons, so flowers should have a bigger budget)

● Consider demographics - will you be entertaining children or adults? What is the one common interest here?

● Find vendors

Depending on how you feel about the environment, finding a vendor may be rather difficult. Some of the decorations will not need a vendor but rather can be made yourself. This is also something you may want to take into consideration.

Do It Yourself

The infamous DIY, which everyone loves but not everyone knows quite how to go about implementing. If you do decide to do a few DIYs here and there for your event, there are plenty of things to prepare for before even starting the construction process. Again, considering your demographic and theme is one of the top things you will need to think about before choosing a DIY. Some events will not be appropriate for DIYs unless you happen to be a professional in these types of things, such as a woodworker. For some people or events, this will be impossible, especially in a short time span.

DIYs are considered to be cheaper than buying the finished product; however many people find that after purchasing the proper equipment for higher-end DIYs that they spend more money.

This is another thing you will need to consider. At the very least, you will need ample time to create the DIYs and they should be started as soon as possible, especially if they are larger or complex and you need to make many of them. DIYs are a great way to make an event more personal, and if you are or know a crafter then you can end up with a very unique and perfect event setup. DIYs allow you to have full customization control, and you can change your course as needed while building to better fit your event.

For many people, DIYs are often the perfect way to go, even if it isn't for every decoration. DIYing things such as centerpieces or invites are a great way to start for someone who wants a few personalized items there but doesn't have the time to make everything themselves.

Setting Up

Setting up the decorations and the layout can be very difficult. You should have someone in charge of directing the others around to make sure everyone places the objects in the correct spaces, as well as having extra hands to help. Hiring some people will be a major help, but you should also search within family or friends for people who want to volunteer their time. You will also want to keep track of who is doing what, and probably have some sort of very rough sketch of the layout and where everything will be put for tracking.

Tracking

Keeping track of what items should go where and who is organizing them is another essential to the event. Making sure an item isn't out of place keeps the layout clear, and making sure you know who is doing what keeps everyone organized. Keeping a spreadsheet and sketch of the layout will make sure you have everything together, and keeps you from overbooking anyone with tasks. Your spreadsheet can simply have the names of the teams or the people, their tasks, and what else is left to do. Your "sketch" of the area really only needs the basic layout, and then a few circles or squares that are labeled as the objects. You can check off each one after they are done for quick tracking.

Your Team

Your team size will vary depending on how many decorations, tables, and general help is needed within the location, as well as the location's size. You should have one to two people who are managers, and then people put into groups to organize the area. Simply, you will need:

● 1-2 Managers, who will overlook the teams and can clearly communicate where items should be put and how.

● Small teams (if possible, can be 1-2 people) to organize items and work together. Remember to only give tasks individuals are able to do.

Decorations and your general setup are some of the main features for any event, and it is especially important to make them comfortable for other people. Decorations can help set up an area even more, and organize and set the tone of the place. However, it can be a little difficult if you aren't entirely sure what you are doing. Nevertheless, building up a team with some foreplanning is the best way you can make sure that setup and decorations become an easier process that guests are sure to love.

Chapter 9

Gifts & goody bags

The final touch on your event – and not every event has one – is the gift or goody bag. This is my favorite part of an event and a little part of me mourns any time the budget doesn't stretch that far or the client doesn't want them. This is what your guests take home with them, other than wonderful memories. To be honest, at a great event, most people won't miss these if you choose not to have them. (I am an exception.) But if you want an event to have a lasting impact, one that people will talk about after they leave other than "It was nice…", the gift bag is the way to do it. It can be simple or it can be elaborate, and that should really match the event itself.

By now you know that my process is to plan big and then scale back. That remains my method for the gift bag, but by the time you get to planning the gift bag, your budget is starting to looking a little thin. And by the time the partygoer receives it, they're preparing to transition from the event, sometimes reluctantly and sometimes because they have elsewhere to be. So you need to make an impression with it – it's the last memory the guest takes out the door and you don't want it to look like the afterthought you ran out of money on. Feel free to dream big on the gift bag, but don't get attached to any ideas. In the end, it may be the thing that gets axed. Even when that isn't the case, it usually gets a massive overhaul a few times over and is often the most creatively frugal part of the event!

Budget

The financial aspect of the goody bag is tricky! If you have a guest list of 50 people, your gift bag expense can easily be $1000 if you aren't careful. Basically, the way I usually figure out a gift bag budget is that I try to be as frugal as possible – without appearing to be frugal – with the overall budget a client gives me, and the leftover amount goes to the goody bags. If the guest list is 20 and the leftovers are $1000, we're going to have a memorable parting gift for sure. If the leftovers are $100 and the guest list is 200, at the very least we'll make sure to leave a bowl of chocolates and a happy helper full of smiles and thank yous by the door on the way out!

Be conscious of whether you want a gift bag from the beginning. That will determine how attached you get to other aspects of the events because this budget definitely runs up if you have the flexibility. You have to plan the materials and content, the packaging, fillers, and the little things like stickers or tags.

If you're planning a home party for a child, a secret I have found to make for incredible gift bags is to plan them over the year from the previous party and buy bags of goodies here and there. Ignorance is bliss, and if you're buying a $20 bag of Halloween candy marked down to use for a party in March, no one has to know the difference and neither does your budget. How often do you throw away $20 without noticing? You can fill those gift bags with random stockpiles over the year with no problem – the back to school sale has cute pencils and stickers and cute Christmas stocking stuffers can be taken advantage of too. Valentine's Day and Easter have fun items that go on sale too. Use your creativity – not just in the stuffing of the bag but in accounting too, if need be!

The Contents

A goody bag needs a minimum of three items, just to be interesting at all. What those items are, how significant they are, and what their quality is, will be determined by both the event and the budget. I've received goody bags at lavish events with five or more items each worth around $100, and I've attended children's events with goody bags that contained a lollipop, a pencil, and a 25 cent bouncy ball.

Back to the budget, let's put those contents in perspective. Say the lollipop is $1 and so is the pencil, and the bouncy ball comes from a quarter machine. The bag they come in is 50 cents and maybe there's a sticker on the bag or a thank you card inside that cost another 25 cents. It seems frugal, right? That's $3 per bag, but if there are 50 kids at the party that's $150 just for that! That's why you have to be very careful with the budget, and if, in the end, you can't make it work with a bang but instead with a sad whimper – resort to that bowl of chocolates and a big smile instead.

But that said, the contents need to reflect the type of event you are throwing. If It's a tech convention with a lot of high rollers or a luxury wedding, you want a gift bag and you want it to have an incredible Wow! factor. If it's a child's fourth birthday party, a few candies, a sticker, and a plastic baggie full of homemade play dough you made for a couple of pennies per bag will probably satisfy every child.

Honor the theme. Is it a business expo? Make sure the products come from vendors and sponsors. A beach wedding might feature an engraved seashell, or a beach-scented candle, or an hourglass of beach sand. A child's party should maintain the theme of the party – for example, if your three-year-old asked for a Paw Patrol party, those candies could be dog-bone shaped and the sticker could be from the show.

Choosing the Packaging

The packaging can be a simple brown paper bag or tissue paper for a small goody bag, or it can be a designer tote bag or purse filled with goodies. I've sadly never been the recipient, but I've seen designer handbags full of fine make-up and Tiffany jewelry. I've received Adidas duffle bags with new seasonal athletic gear and elaborate gift box structures that look like they were designed by engineers full of candies.

Don't forget the packaging when figuring your budget for goody bags, and make the packaging as nice as you can without going beyond your means. For smaller and less formal events, particularly with less mature patrons, the most important factor is simply that it contains all the goodies inside!

Putting Together Your Bags

It's easy and completely fine to put off putting together gift bags until the very end of the party preparations. If you have an extra set of hands, it doesn't even matter if they're not put together until the party is in full swing. Simply put the materials and supplies to the side and work on them as you can. To begin with, just prep enough packaging for the number of guests you have. That means, don't save the packaging for last! It gets set up first. Then start placing items in, piece by piece. Obviously, if any of the contents are do-it-yourself, you'll want to get started on those at least a week in advance, depending on your free time and the elaborateness of the craft. Once they're filled, close them up with a sticker or a ribbon. Put the gift bags aside and out of sight until it's time to give them to guests!

Gift bags are the final touch, both literally and figuratively in the event. They aren't a necessity, but they're a favorite. Don't feel bad when you have to skip them altogether but use your creativity to make them as creative and bountiful as possible!

Chapter 10

Day before and day of set-up

The days before the event are when showtime really begins. Depending on where you host the event and how formal it is, you can really begin the work of the "day before" several days in advance. This is the time to put up decorations, make sure the food is prepped and ready, make sure all volunteer and paid helpers (or forced helpers, if they're family, let's be honest) are prepped in their roles, rearrange furniture, pick up last-minute items, and get everything perfect before the guests show up.

Your Crew

Get in touch with everyone who is planning to help with the event. Make sure you know where you need help and assign everyone a role. If the event is formal enough that it requires a schedule, run through the schedule for any flaws. Give everyone their assignments and let them know when to arrive, how they need to dress, what they need to bring, and so on. Answer any questions they might have.

The most important advice I can give you in this particular area is if anyone sounds unsure they will be there, listen to the unsaid message they send, even if they swear they will be there. If they don't want to be there, they most likely will magically come down with an emergency or illness on the day of the event – it isn't even necessarily conscious or intended. Then you'll be (at least) one man down and in crisis. Request more helpers than you need and if you get the idea someone is waffling, prepare for someone to take their place.

Be clear about what each person's role is. Otherwise, they'll stand around with a lot to do but no idea where to start, nervous about jumping into your personal chaos. Be aware that's how humans work and have assignments ready for them to jump into.

Food

The day before the party, make sure you have everything ready for the menu – what has been premade, plus the ingredients for whatever can only be made the day of. Make sure all serving items are available and easily accessible. Plan where you will put the food, what time it needs to be out, and what preparation needs to be done in advance to make all that happen. Make sure there are plenty of plates, cups, utensils, and napkins, and whatever else will be needed for your menu as well. Also, don't forget strategically placed trash cans and trash bags;

otherwise your party will start looking like a garbage dump fast.

Decorations and Furniture

The day before the party, you can start hanging decorations. Make sure you have whatever implements you need for this – tape, glue sticks, and glue guns, staples, nails, hammers, and so on. Other than fresh flowers, balloons, or food items, anything can go out the day before. Whatever goes on walls or hangs from ceilings should go up first – in other words, whatever is out of the way and gets some of your stack of party stuff out of your way, too.

Then put out the tables, complete with table covers and centerpieces. If there are table settings, you can go ahead and put these out as well. Wait to put out chairs until everything else is done because they'll get in your way.

Make sure you set out a gift table! Even if It's not an event requiring a gift, many people bring thank you or host gifts, so set everything aside, with a notebook and pen on the table to record who gave you what. You'll want to thank everyone later!

Equipment

Do you have a band playing or need audio? Go ahead and set it up. If you have someone coming in, meaning it's not your equipment readily available, you can at least reserve the space for them. They'll come in and set up when it's the agreed-upon time and you don't have to worry about anything.

Last Minute Decorations

I try to finish the décor the day before, except anything involving food (ice sculptures or fountains, fruit displays, and so on), fresh flowers, or balloons. Any battery-operated lighting should wait until just before the event as well. Once everything is in place, take a look around. Is there anything missing? If it's something you completely forgot about, it's a good thing you got everything ready the day before! You have the evening and the next morning to get everything finished. If it's something you simply forgot to put out, grab it and be done. Look around for empty spaces or anything that just doesn't look good and needs to be rethought. You have time right now to problem-solve.

The Day of the Event

Get all the food ready! That's number one on the list today! Be prepared enough in advance so that it's all out when guests start arriving and you're not still running around. Know exactly what you need to run out for in the morning and get it done as quickly and efficiently as possible. Get back and put out those last décor items that wouldn't maintain their perk the day before. Set up any games and other events that would have gotten in the way the day before. Be ready for your vendors to start to show up. Make time to be prepared yourself! Then be ready to greet guests!

Conclusion

By the time your event is over, you're probably exhausted and you just want to relax! There are two schools of thought – either relax and worry about the clean-up tomorrow, or get everything set up and back to normal immediately. This is where you're going to wish you chose another place to hold the event if you didn't do that, that's a normal part of the process and at-home events are still some of the best and most personal festivities.

I'm of the school that you should force yourself into a fast burst of energy and get the trash cleaned up immediately. You can put off deep cleaning or dishwashing if you don't have it in you, but at the very least, get the trash out and pull down any decorations and put away as much of the extra furnishings as you can. Keep going until you don't have any energy left – but at the minimum, get the trash out, and put everything back in its "zone". The zone means that dishes go back into the kitchen, even if that means piled up on the sink. Food too, but put that away completely so it doesn't get ruined.

File away the notebook with the gift list, but not so far away that you won't be able to pull it out in a couple of days to write the thank-you notes. – Does anyone still thank you notes? You should! Be the exception if you think they don't. People don't have to participate to make your day a success, and they bring gifts just for the honor of it! Get the notes out within 3 days; they can be electronic if you have everyone's email address or they're on your Facebook profile.

Upload any photos immediately; otherwise, it might be weeks before life slows down again and no one is interested in seeing them anymore! If you're exhausted at this point, you can wait for the day after the event to put away furniture and equipment. Return any rented or borrowed items immediately to prevent grudges or late fees.

Now you've gone from being completely overwhelmed planning a small event to being a pro at hosting a flawless one, right? Just kidding – don't ever fool yourself into believing it will be quite that easy – even the pros have at least one problem, sometimes of disastrous proportions, at a lot of events. It gets easier over time but it's always an adventure. This guide is intended to prevent the biggest problems and help you brainstorm how to solve the little ones that inevitably arise. I hope it has helped you harness all the ideas for your event and funnel them into a practical and deliverable day that will be successful beyond your wildest dreams!

One last thing!

I want to give you a **one-in-two-hundred chance** to win a **$200.00 Amazon Gift card** as a thank-you for reading this book.

All I ask is that you give me some feedback, so I can improve this or my next book :)

Your opinion is *super valuable* to me. It will only take a minute of your time to let me know what you like and what you didn't like about this book. The hardest part is deciding how to spend the two hundred dollars! Just follow this link.

http://reviewers.win/smallevent

Checklists and timelines

Party Supply Checklist

Decorations
banners
signs
streamers
balloons
tape
glue guns
glue sticks

Table Settings
plates and bowls
cups
napkins
silverware
straws and stirrers

Favors
favor toys/contents
favor bags/boxes
cupcake bags
sticker/ribbon

Table Decorations
tablecloth
placemat
table runner
chair cover
centerpieces
seating chart signage
chair decorations

Serving Pieces
cake stand
serving dishes
vases
trays
serving pieces

Paper
invitations
welcome sign
cake topper
food tents

Event Timeline Checklist

One Month Before

- ❑ Set the budget
- ❑ Choose theme
- ❑ Set time
- ❑ Choose location
- ❑ Create guest list
- ❑ Order invitations
- ❑ Book vendors

Three Weeks Before

- ❑ Plan decorations
- ❑ Shopping list
- ❑ To-do list
- ❑ Send invitations
- ❑ Plan menu
- ❑ Decide on a party outfit
- ❑ Recruit help

Two Weeks Before

- ❑ Test run the DIYs
- ❑ Order decorations
- ❑ Order favors

One Week Before

- ❏ Shop for groceries
- ❏ Plan playlist
- ❏ Find serving dishes and utensils
- ❏ Shop for supplies
- ❏ Bake & freeze cake
- ❏ Stock goody bags
- ❏ Confirm vendors
- ❏ Complete any DIYs
- ❏ Write out schedule
- ❏ Finalize headcount
- ❏ Start cooking
- ❏ Stock the bar

Three Days Before

- ❏ Test run food displays
- ❏ Remove personal items from public places (medicine cabinet etc)
- ❏ Find a place for coats and purses
- ❏ Washing serving dishes and utensils

Two Days Before

- ❏ Clean the house
- ❏ Prep cameras
- ❏ Check for toilet paper/paper towels
- ❏ Pick up rentals
- ❏ Purchase perishables

- ❑ Reconfirm vendors
- ❑ Confirm help

One Day Before

- ❑ Set up furniture
- ❑ Defrost cake
- ❑ Set up games/activities
- ❑ Finish cooking
- ❑ Decorations
- ❑ Clean bathroom

Day of the Party

- ❑ Final decor
- ❑ Buy ice
- ❑ Frost cake or pick it up
- ❑ Display food and drinks
- ❑ Place trash cans

How much food do I need

Appetizers	6 bites before a meal 4-6/hour if as meal	per person
Main course	Meat 8 oz Grain 15 oz Potatoes 5 oz Veggies and fruit 4 oz Salad 1 oz	per person
Drinks	Wine ½ bottle Beer 2 bottles/hour Soft drinks 24 oz Water ⅓ liter	per person
Desserts	1 slice cake 5 oz ice cream 3 oz ice cream w/ cake 3 cookies	per person

Rules to observe:

- Purchase more white wine than red.

- Use a lot of bread and cheese to cover accidental understocks.

- Round up on any estimates.

- Order more of any crowd favorites.

- Have someone on call to make food runs if stock runs
  low.